# Kirkbymoorside

10 WALKS 6 MILES OR LESS

Dalesman

Dalesman Publishing Company Ltd
Stable Courtyard, Broughton Hall,
Skipton, North Yorkshire BD23 3AZ

First Edition 1999

Text © Nick Channer

Illustrations © Christine Isherwood:
p5 wren, p15 foxglove, p16 wild daffodils, p24 elderberries,
p29 bullfinch

Maps by Jeremy Ashcroft

Cover : Hutton-le-Hole near Kirkbymoorside by Roger Kilvington

A British Library Cataloguing in Publication record
is available for this book

ISBN 1 85568 160 9

Printed by Amadeus Press, Huddersfield

Contents

Introduction

Sheltering beneath heather-clad moorland, Kirkbymoorside is a quiet little town with a broad, cobble-edged main street climbing steadily between sturdy Georgian houses and lines of shop fronts. One of Kirkbymoorside's oldest buildings is the Black Swan, which boasts an elaborately carved entrance porch dated 1632. The town is recorded in the Domesday Book, though Kirkbymoorside's roots date back to prehistoric times. The parish church was rebuilt in the 19th century.

Above the town, between familiar windswept ridges, glorious green dales fan out to the north. A springtime stroll in Farndale reveals drifts of golden daffodils as far as the eye can see, a magical sight to lift the spirits, while the two walks at Gillamoor and Fadmoor offer frequent glimpses of some of the national park's most spectacular scenery.

Hutton-le-Hole, nestling in the Tabular Hills, is the starting point for an exhilarating walk across unspoilt, pastoral landscapes, with good views over tracts of rolling countryside. The village is the setting for the Ryedale Folk Museum, which depicts rural life as it used to be in previous centuries and is one of the region's most popular attractions. Appleton-le-Moors, Cropton and Wrelton all lie to the north of the A170 and from these villages you can explore tracts of spectacular, varied countryside close to the southern entrance to Rosedale.

South of Kirkbymoorside, the character and appearance of the region change abruptly. Immediately you leave the town you find yourself in the fertile Vale of Pickering, heading across expansive, lowland country characterized by a vast network of field patterns, trees and hedgerows. During the last Ice Age this entire area was under water with the remains of decaying vegetation settling on the lake floor to form good quality soil. Deep in this rural landscape is the village of Marton where you can begin a delightfully pastoral walk across country to neighbouring Normanby, returning to the start via a stretch of the Seven riverbank.

Pockley and Riccal Dale

Length of walk: 3¹/₂ miles
Start/finish: Pockley village centre, north of the A170 between Helmsley and Kirkbymoorside
Terrain: Easy road walking on the outward leg, with a mixture of woodland paths and tracks on the return. Parts of the route can be rather overgrown in summer

This circular walk begins in the quiet village of Pockley and then explores one of the North York Moors National Park's lesser-known dales.

From Pockley church walk up the lane, heading north out of the village. Rows of picturesque stone cottages line the road before it cuts between West Farm on the left and Manor Farm on the right. Pass a turning for Bedlam Rigg on the right and continue along Northfield Lane, a no through road which eventually dwindles to a track at Birk Nab Farm. This stretch of the walk offers expansive views over desolate countryside and open moorland, their bleakness in places relieved only by bursts of woodland and sprawling conifer plantations.

On the far horizon lies Bransdale, one of the loneliest of the dales that cut deep into the North York Moors. Here, the landscape is dotted with red-tiled farmhouses, and tracts of heather moorland, unchanged by the passage of time, echo to the sound of curlews, red grouse and lapwings. The unfenced road leads through the dale to the tiny village of Cockayne, whose houses and cottages are situated either side of the valley road. According to legend, Cockayne is a mythical place of luxury and indolence.

Follow the quiet lane between fields and hedgerows, with grand views of the national park continuing to dominate the scene. Up ahead now are the buildings of Oxclose Farm. Pass the farm and continue on the road until it starts to curve a little to the right, at the point where it becomes fenced. Turn left where there are wooden gates either side of the road and follow the grassy bridleway towards some trees. The rolling, tree-clad slopes of remote Riccal Dale can be seen climbing to the distant skyline. The track curves left in the field corner to reach a second gate. Pass through it and keep ahead. When, after about 75 yards, the track sweeps away to the right and down the slope, continue straight on through a wooden gate.

Follow the path along the woodland edge and on the right, between the trees, are teasing glimpses of Riccal Dale. On a still day, the only sound to disturb the acute silence here is likely to be that of pheasants scurrying nervously through the undergrowth as you approach. Keep to the rutted, grassy track, muddy in places after prolonged rain, and eventually a footpath sign edges into view ahead. Veer half left at this point and follow the path between carpets of bracken and alongside trees on the edge of the woodland. There are pleasant views across farmland over to the left. Avoid a path running down into the trees and undergrowth on the right and continue to skirt the woodland, the overhanging branches of the trees providing welcome shade on a warm, sunny day.

Descend quite steeply to a gate and the site of a disused quarry on the left. Cross the track and go up the bank following the signposted footpath to a stile. Cut through an area of bracken and, once clear of it, head down the field slope to a footpath sign. The trees of Riccal Dale are a short distance away to the right. Follow the grassy path across scrub ground, with a dilapidated wall on the left. When the path curves to the right towards woodland, go straight on through bracken. The vague outline of a path can be identified here. Follow it between bushes, bracken and banks of vegetation.

Eventually you come to a gate. Pass through it and keep ahead, crossing another area of scrub. Go through a galvanized gate and keep on the track as it curves to the left at a junction. There are striking views to distant horizons as you complete the final stage of the track. Pass through a gate, turn left and return to the centre of Pockley.

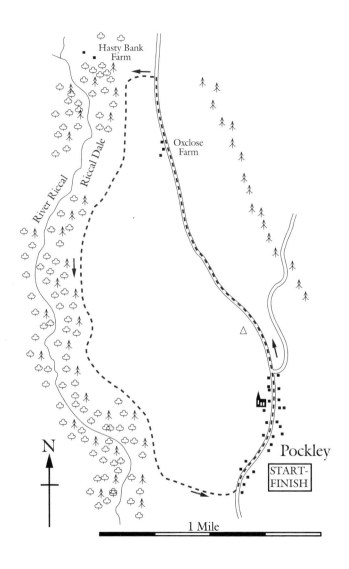

Hasty Bank
Farm

River Riccal

Riccal Dale

Oxclose
Farm

N

Pockley

START-
FINISH

1 Mile

Wombleton

Length of walk: 2¹/₂ miles
Start/finish: Wombleton village centre, south of the A170, midway between Kirkbymoorside and Helmsley
Terrain: Tracks, field paths and a stretch of country road

Easy circular walk revealing good views of the intricate field patterns to the west of the village of Wombleton.

Located in the Vale of Pickering, the village of Wombleton is characterized by its mix of architectural styles. Rows of sturdy stone cottages stand alongside modern houses and bungalows. However, Wombleton's origins are medieval, as its single main street and field patterns clearly indicate. Several buildings are of cruck construction.

From the centre of Wombleton head north, following the main street towards the A170. Turn left into Back Lane on the outskirts of the village and when the road bends left after several yards, go right to a stile. Go straight across to the opposite corner of the field, then follow the boundary to the next corner. Keep ahead, with a hedge on the right, making for the next corner. Avoid a path on the right and go straight on, keeping to the left of a thick hedgerow. Cross another stile after about 50 yards and then continue ahead between hedges, fences, bushes and trees. Pass a farm on the right and bend right towards the village of Nawton.

Continue on the tarmac lane, following it between hedgerows, and pass a footpath and some stone cottages on the right. Turn left and walk alongside Calverts factory to join a path running alongside a drive leading to several chalets. Go through a kissing gate and head diagonally across the field to reach a kissing gate in the boundary. Head straight down the next field to a white cottage, turn left and follow Gale Lane as it heads south out of Nawton. Pass Ryedale School and a glance at the surroundings here reveals very pleasant views over gentle, farming landscapes.

Follow the road round several bends and continue between trees and hedgerows. Pass the entrance to a caravan and camp site on the right and follow the road for about 120 yards, turning left into Syke Lane. Keep to the broad track, which is also a public footpath, and follow it between trees and extensive rural landscapes. Pass the buildings of Syke House Farm and keep going for about 80 yards until you reach a gate and footpath sign in the left boundary. Go straight down the field slope Swing right on reaching the corner of the woodland on the right and make for two stiles and a footbridge spanning the Syke Cut on the far side of the field. Cross the field on the opposite side of the cut and make for a stile and footbridge by some trees. Veer diagonally left across the field and join a path skirting the boundary. Keep trees and hedgerow on the left and ahead are the buildings of Wombleton. Look for a gap in the left boundary and cross into the neighbouring field. Pass under power lines and between clumps of thistles to reach a stile in the far right corner.

Follow a short section of path to join a grassy track and walk ahead, keeping the houses of Wombleton on the right. Keep going when Back Lane becomes a metalled road and follow it round to the right to the main junction. Turn right for the centre of Wombleton.

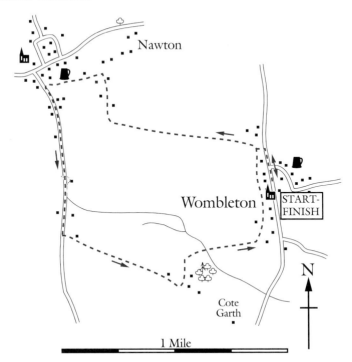

Fadmoor

Length of walk: 2¹/₂ miles
Start/finish: Fadmoor village centre, 2 miles north of Kirkbymoorside
Terrain: Extensive stretches of field path, some road walking. One quite steep ascent out of the valley. Wet and muddy in places

Short walk across open farmland with grand views of Kirk Dale and Sleightholme Dale. Fadmoor, which lies at the entrance to Farndale, boasts a pretty village green, picturesque houses and a classic English pub.

Starting at the green in Fadmoor, keep The Plough on the right and walk out of the village towards Kirkbymoorside. Take the turning on the right for Sleightholme Dale and Welburn and follow the road between hedegrows. Keep going until you see a stile and footpath sign in the right-hand boundary. Cross into the field, pass through a gate, turn left and follow the field boundary, keeping the wire fence on your left. Continue across this exposed, windswept farmland for some time, passing a solitary tree. Eventually you reach the field corner where there is a gate and waymark. Go straight ahead across the next field, still keeping hard by the boundary. There are superb views ahead of Kirk Dale.

Cross a stile in the bottom boundary of the field, drop down the bank to the road and turn right. Walk along a pretty stretch of lane, following it between bushes and under the branches of overhanging trees. The lane winds through dense woodland for some time and occasionally you are treated to fine views.

Further down the road, pass a footpath sign for Hold Caldron and at this point you are treated to a magnificent view of lush pastures cowering beneath steep, tree-clad slopes. To extend the walk, follow the signposted path through Kirk Dale, keeping close to the meandering Hodge Beck, and after nearly 2 miles you reach Hold Caldron. Keep going for another mile and you reach St Gregory's Minster, a gem of a church that makes this lengthy detour truly worth the effort. Hidden away in secluded Kirk Dale, sheltered by trees, this ancient building was dedicated to St Gregory, the first monk to become Pope. The original church on this site was sacked by Danish invaders in the mid-9th century and subsequently rebuilt. According to some historians, St Cedd, who, on leaving Lindisfarne in the 7th century, chose nearby Lastingham as the site for a monastery, is buried beneath St Gregory's Minster. One of the best examples of a Saxon sundial can be seen in the porch of St Gregory's Minster, built in the 19th century.

From the church retrace your steps through Kirk Dale, join the road and pass alongside Sleightholme Dale Cottages. Beyond them is the entrance to Sleightholme Dale Lodge, the grounds enclosed by a high stone wall. Follow the lane beside a hedge. As you approach farm outbuildings at Aumery Park, turn sharp right at a gate and head up the grassy hillside under some power cables. Make for clumps of gorse bushes and enter a wood further up the slope.

Ascend to a gate and continue through the undergrowth, picking your way between gorse bushes. The path curves a little to the right to reach a stile. Cross it and go diagonally across the field to a stile. Turn left and cross six fields via a series of stiles. Eventually you reach the road, approaching it between a house and farm outbuildings. Turn right to return to the centre of Fadmoor. The village hall can be seen on the right.

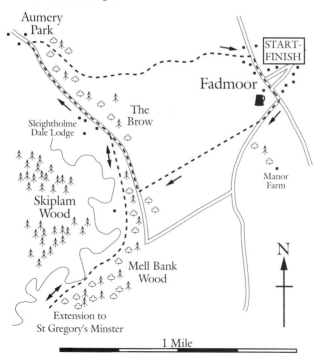

Surprise View

Length of walk: 6 miles
Start/finish: Lay-by in Highfield Lane, nearly 1 mile north-west of
Gillamoor. The village lies about 2 miles north of Kirkbymoorside
Terrain: Plenty of tree cover, stretches of exposed moorland and open
countryside. Several climbs, including one steep ascent

The lofty village of Gillamoor is probably best known for its Surprise View, a popular vantage point at the top of the escarpment. From here the walk descends to the River Dove, exploring a thickly wooded stretch of the valley, part of the Farndale Nature Reserve, before striking out over Harland Moor, from where there are impressive views across Farndale.

Look for a footpath sign and gate opposite the lay-by and head diagonally left across the field, aiming for the right-hand edge of a line of trees. Follow the path as it skirts the field, with a belt of woodland, known as The Storth, on the left. Pass through a dilapidated gate and keep to the path as it runs just inside the woodland. Continue ahead, with a hint of Gillamoor's timeless Surprise View through the trees.

The path cuts between margins of bracken and vegetation, including cow parsley and many different wild flowers and plants, to reach a seat on the left, conveniently placed to take advantage of the magnificent view. Turn right at the road to visit Gillamoor.

Gillamoor, guarding the entrance to Farndale, once included a blacksmith's forge, garage, two stonemasons and a billiards room. Mostly, it is a quiet community today, though the summer months bring a convoy of visitors and sightseers who come to admire its airy green around which are clustered groups of sturdy houses and cottages. The rare four-faced sundial, dating back to 1800, is among Gillamoor's more unusual features. Located in the centre of the village, it can be found close to the remains of the old pound.

After a brief tour of the village follow the Hutton-le-Hole road, passing the church on the right. On reaching the Gillamoor sign, 'Surprise View' greets the eye.

Surprise View, as it has come to be known over the years, was once a favourite vantage point for watching the trail hounds, some of which were kennelled in Gillamoor. Today, it is the Sinnington foxhounds, in pursuit of

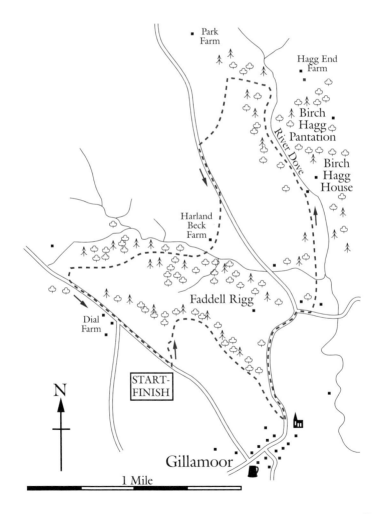

their quarry, which attract the crowds. Note the words of J Keble, inscribed on a plaque in the wall by the seat.

> " Thou, who hast given me eyes to see
> And love this sight so fair.. "

A seat enables passers-by to relax and appreciate this glorious scene. Follow the lane down through the trees and then round to the right. Pass a track to Faddell Rigg Farm followed by a turning for Farndale and continue towards Hutton-le-Hole. Turn left (signposted Lowna car park), and walk through the parking area, passing beneath power lines. Follow a dirt track towards some trees, part of Farndale Nature Reserve.

Cross the Harland Beck via the footbridge. The next stretch of the walk includes the site of a Quaker burial ground. At the junction of routes just beyond the beck, take the left path (signposted Low Mill via Park Farm) and keep to the right when the path forks at a waymark. Follow the path, with a stone wall on the right and good views over the nature reserve.

On reaching a gate and a waymark, turn right and descend the slope, keeping the woodland on the left. Turn left, at a junction of paths further down, taking the lower of the two parallel paths. Follow the path as it carves a passage through a luxuriant carpet of heather and bracken, with the meandering River Dove just a stone's throw to the right.

Merge with another path and continue beside the river before reaching a gate and Dale End Bridge. Do not cross the river. Instead, turn left and leave this delightfully wooded, waterside stretch of the walk by climbing steeply out of the valley, keeping a fence on the left. Pass under some power lines, crossing a track to a stile. Continue ascending the slopes, following the path as it weaves through the heather and bracken. Having emerged now from the tree cover, there is a wonderful sense of space on this higher ground, with grand views right across Farndale.

Cross a stile and a track to reach a second track after several yards. Turn left and follow it over Harland Moor. Take care when walking here. Even the softest of footsteps on this open ground can flush grouse out of the heather with alarming abruptness. Follow the track to the road and turn left. Bear right at the next bridleway sign, entering the field via the gate. Turn left after about 15 yards into the adjacent field. Cross it to the far boundary, with the buildings of Harland Beck Farm ahead.

Pass through a gate and cross the next field, keeping a wall on the left. Make for a gate to the left of the farm outbuildings and cross the main drive to join a visible path running round to the right. With the farmhouse over to the right, cross the Harland Beck once more and then bear right, through a gate. This section of the walk can be somewhat overgrown in places during the summer months. Follow the path up the slope and soon it hugs a fence on the right. Veer left at a bridleway sign and follow the path through the woodland. Turn left at the next track and follow it for about 80 yards to the next junction.

Bear right and follow the track through open farmland. Pass through a gate, with a sign —'keep dogs on leads', and continue on the bridleway as it runs between fences. On reaching some double gates and a stile, turn left and follow the bridleway up the slope to the road. Bear left and head up through the trees. Pass Donhill Farm and keep left at the fork (signposted Gillamoor 1 mile). Return to the lay-by where the walk began.

Farndale Daffodil Walk

Length of walk: 3 miles
**Start/finish: Low Mill car park north of Kirkbymoorside and Gillamoor. To
avoid crowds and traffic congestion, it is recommended that walkers
undertaking this route avoid weekends and bank holidays in spring
Type of walk: A gentle walk, initially following field paths and tracks along
the eastern flank of Farndale, returning to Low Mill along the valley floor**

*Farndale's famous riverside walk, thickly strewn with wild daffodils for a few
short weeks during March and April, is on every visitor's itinerary, and even
local residents annually visit the dale to cherish the image and memory of this
dazzling scene. This walk saves the best until the end. Beginning at Low Mill, it
journeys across open farmland, along the slopes of Farndale, to a secret church
hidden among the trees. From here the route makes for the banks of the River
Dove and its final objective —the magical Farndale Daffodil Walk.*

On leaving the car park at Low Mill, which takes its name from two corn mills,
turn immediately right at a gate and head down to a second gate followed by a
footbridge spanning the River Dove. Once over the river,
avoid the riverside path on the left, representing the
return leg of the walk, and go straight ahead into the
field. Keep roughly parallel to some power lines, with
a hedge on the right. At the hedge corner, continue
ahead on the trod to a stile in the fence and trees.

Cross it to another stile and keep going in the next
field, with a wall on the left. On reaching a farm,
pass through a gate into the farmyard, bear
immediately left and follow the track between
hedgerows. There are glorious views across Farndale at
this point. As the track curves left into a field, go straight
on through a gate and up the slope, following the field
boundary and keeping alongside the hedge.

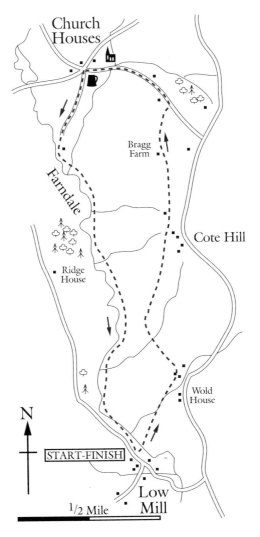

Church
Houses

Farndale

Bragg
Farm

Cote Hill

Ridge
House

Wold
House

N

START-FINISH

Low
Mill

$^1/_2$ Mile

Pass through a gate in the field corner and bear right, skirting the field. Make for a gate in the top right-hand corner and continue keeping to the right-hand boundary, heading for the farm at Cote Hill. The craggy outcrop of Taylor's Nab, on the edge of Low Blakey Moor, rises to the right of it. Pass through another gate and then veer left just before reaching the farm outbuildings.

Follow a vague track round the side of the buildings and now make for a ladder-stile over to the left. Cross it and keep the wall on the right. Cross another stile and walk straight ahead towards another farm. Pass through a gate, keep the farmhouse on the left and follow the track as it bends to the right. At this point, cross the stile into the field and follow the vague outline of a path.

Join a track and follow it towards Bragg Farm. On reaching a sign for Mackeridge, go straight on between the farm outbuildings, through a gate and past another footpath sign. Make for the next field boundary where there are gates either side of a hedge. Take the gate on the right and then cross a ladder-stile ahead in the field corner. Bear right and follow the wall along to the road.

Turn left, pass a solitary house as the lane curves left and continue down towards Church Houses, with the hills rising like protective guardians above the buildings of this small community. At this stage of the walk, it is worth stopping to have a look at Farndale's church of St Mary, which occupies a solitary, peaceful setting hidden from the road. The entrance to the church can be seen on the right just before Church Houses.   Rebuilt after Bransdale and Farndale became separate parishes in 1871, the church was again renovated after the First World War. Among several notable features is the large chancel with its fine timber roof. There has been a place of Christian workship on this site for a thousand years.

Walk through the hamlet and on the left is a welcome pub, the Fevisham Arms. From the inn turn left and take the 'no through road' down through the fields to a gate. Continue along the track, avoiding the turning to Cow Bank on the right, and head towards 'Poppy's Pantry'. Walk between the buildings of High Mill to a gate. A sign here advises walkers that the Farndale estate is owned by Sir Lawrence Barrett, of 'Barrett Homes' fame, and that 'he wishes all visitors to enjoy the peace and tranquillity of the dale.'

During the spring, this stretch of the walk, as far south as Low Mill, attracts hordes of visitors, as many as 40,000 a year, who come to marvel at the spectacular carpet of daffodils, which grow in colourful profusion along the banks of the River Dove. Some sources claim it is the elements that have dispersed the flowers over a 6 mile/9.5 km area, while others attribute their planting to the monks of Rievaulx.

Follow the path across tree-fringed meadows and through several bursts of light woodland. There are constant views of Farndale and the River Dove is just a stone's throw to the right. Because of the volume of visitors on this stretch, stiles have been replaced by gates.   Pass a pond and a weir and on reaching a footbridge, cross to the opposite bank, go through a gate and follow the path up to the car park at Low Mill.

Hutton-le-Hole and Spaunton

Length of walk: 4¹/₄ miles
Start/finish: Hutton-le-Hole is about 2 miles north of the A170
between Kirkbymoorside and Pickering. Car park at northern end
of village
Terrain: Not physically demanding but a pleasant walk crossing many
pastures and enclosures by paths and tracks

A breezy, exhilarating walk which begins by climbing out of Hutton-le-Hole, then crosses high-level, open farmland before reaching Spaunton village. The return leg, equally spectacular, provides good views across Spaunton Moor, a dark, heathery landscape stretching to the horizon.

Enjoying a sheltered position in the Tabular Hills, Hutton-le-Hole is one of the national park's most visited villages, due in no small part to the award-winning Ryedale Folk Museum which includes a collection of painstakingly re-erected buildings from different periods and depicts village life as it used to be two to three hundred years ago. Hutton Beck runs through the village, meandering between spacious greens and rows of picturesque, limestone cottages. Most of the houses date back to the 17th and 18th centuries, with many of the original residents setting up as spinners and weavers in response to a national demand for cloth, using wool from local moorland sheep. Hutton is an Anglo-Saxon word for farmstead or hamlet — the "le" is a Victorian affectation.

From the car park bear left at the main junction, pass the Crown and Ryedale Folk Museum and walk down to the southern edge of Hutton-le-Hole. Turn left at the sign "keep track clear — access to properties" and follow the lane for about 100 yards. Veer off half left (signposted Cropton) and take the track up the slope and round to the right. The track narrows to a path now. Pass through a gate and walk between trees and banks of

19

undergrowth. The path climbs steadily and further up the trees thin to reveal views over high-level countryside with glimpses of distant woodland and open pasture.

Keep to the path as it bends left and cuts between hedgerows and drystone walls. Bear sharp right and at this stage the path broadens to a track. On reaching some double wooden gates, with Lingmoor Farm visible ahead, turn left to join a grassy bridleway. Descend gently, disregarding a footpath crossing the route of the walk. The bridleway runs quite steeply up through some trees, then veers right to keep just inside the woodland cover.

Eventually the path reaches a gate with some dilapidated barns and farm outbuildings ahead. Bear left here to follow Lingmoor Lane, on a faint grassy track running across the field. Keep a line of trees over to the left and approach a gate. Continue ahead on a much clearer track between trees and hedgerows. On reaching a major junction of tracks, turn left and follow Spaunton Lane.

Pass a footpath on the left and continue on the track towards the village of Spaunton. Negotiate a gate beneath some trees and make for the road junction ahead. To explore the village centre, turn right at this point; otherwise, continue straight ahead.

Note the old North Riding village sign — an unexpected reminder of how the 1974 county boundary alterations changed the map of Britain virtually beyond recognition. Until then Yorkshire was divided into three administrative regions — North Riding, East Riding and West Riding. South Riding existed only in the imagination of the writer Winifred Holtby who used it as the title for her classic novel.

After about 40 yards, bear left at the cattle-grid and public footpath sign. Veer right as you approach Grange Farm and walk between the barns and farm outbuildings. Turn right by a bungalow and then swing left after about 70 yards. Head for some barns; the southern edge of Spaunton Moor is visible over to the right. Turn left by the barns and then take the next track on the right, following the yellow waymark.

Follow the track as it runs in a straight line for some distance. This stage of the walk offers excellent views over a wide, uncluttered landscape. On reaching a bend, where there are glimpses of the buildings of Hutton-le-Hole, with the curtain of Westfield Wood rising above the village, turn left and then bear right after about 70 yards. There is a dilapidated stone byre on the left. Follow the path down through an area of pretty woodland. Pass through an opening in the trees on the right, follow the left-hand boundary of the field down to a gate and descend steeply to the banks of the Fairy Call Beck. Follow the path, strewn with stones and rocks, alongside the beck.

On reaching a yellow waymark, turn left and follow the path to a gate and stile. Cross the grass to the road, turn left for a few strides, then bear sharp right at the sign 'local traffic only'. Follow the lane through Hutton-le-Hole, keeping the main road through the village over to your right. Take the footpath leading down to Hutton Beck. Cross the water to the main road, turn left, then right at the junction and return to the car park.

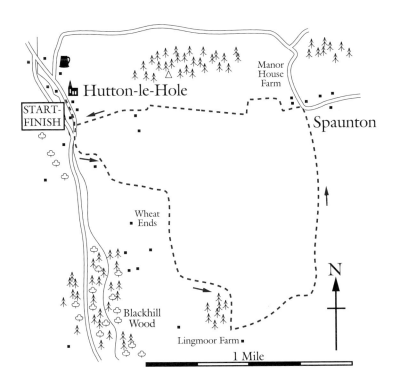

Appleton-le-Moors and Sinnington

Length of walk: 4¹/₂ miles
Start/finish: Appleton-le-Moors, north of the A170 between Pickering and Kirkbymoorside
Terrain: Stretches of quiet lane and track; woodland paths, sometimes wet and muddy; sections of riverside and field paths

Picturesque circular walk following a stretch of the River Seven between the villages of Appleton-le-Moors and Sinnington.

Located just inside the southern boundary of the North York Moors National Park, Appleton-le-Moors is famous for its exceptionally wide main street which, unusually, runs north to south through the village. Christ Church is well worth a look, described by John Betjeman as 'a little gem among moorland churches.' Its remarkable French Gothic style and soaring spire make it a notable local landmark.

Pass Appleton Hall and Christ Church and head north out of Appleton-le-Moors. Take the first right turning (signposted Cropton and Rosedale) and follow the lane between high hedgerows. Pass a footpath on the right and continue to where the road bends left. Go straight on at this point, following the track towards Appleton Mill Farm. Cross a cattle-grid and between the trees are pretty views of the wooded valley of the River Seven. Pass a turning on the right and continue down to the farm which lies beneath a luxuriant curtain of woodland rising to meet the skyline.

As the track bends right towards the farm outbuildings, pass through a gate and go straight ahead, keeping the fence on your right. Follow the path along to the bridge, cross the Seven and turn left. Very soon the path veers away from the river, heading towards a footpath sign at a junction. Turn right and follow the path signposted Sinnington. On the right here is an attractive tree-fringed meadow. Negotiate several gates and follow the path through the woodland to reach a triangular junction. Veer right and head down the slope, keeping to the broad main path. At the next gate, where a white cottage with a striking red roof can be seen

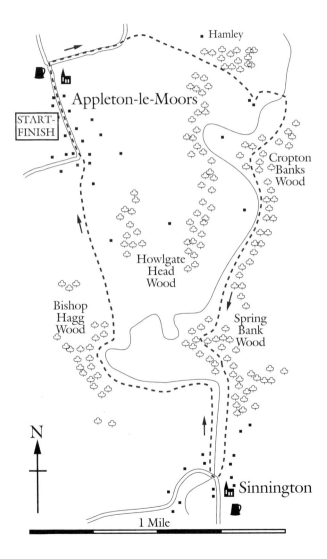

ahead, turn left and follow the path along the woodland edge. There are memorable views of meadows and glorious hanging woods over to the right.

Continue for some time and suddenly the River Seven looms into view. Climb above the river and soon you can see it scurrying away between the trees far below. When the path forks keep to the lower route and eventually you reach a stile on the edge of Hob Bank Wood. Cross over and very soon the path begins to curve right, passing through a gap in the trees. Cross the meadows, strewn with thistles and enclosed by trees along their boundaries, and make for a stile on the far side. Head up the slope, following the track through the trees. The Seven can still be seen dashing through the trees on the right. Keep to the main track as it runs down through the woodland and along a field boundary.

On reaching the Seven once again, continue ahead, avoiding a bridle path running off sharp right. Keep the river close by on the right, follow the lane into Sinnington and make for the village green. A map of the parish rights of way can be seen here.

Close by and looking like some stranded vessel is a 'dry' medieval packhorse bridge spanning a dry ditch which may have once been a flood channel or an old water course. Not far away, up on the hill overlooking the village, lies the church of All Saints, dating back to the 12th century and characterized by a variety of styles. Opposite stands the tithe barn, designated an ancient monument.

Aim for the attractive 18th-century bridge spanning the Seven and cross to the opposite bank. Turn immediately right and follow the riverside bridleway out of the village. Go through a white gate and then follow the path as it bends left in line with the river. Over to the left now are views across open pastures. Keep to the track along the field edge until you reach a gate and a sign for Appleton-le-Moors.

Follow the path for the village; head through the woods and on the right you can just glimpse the River Seven far below. Fed by moorland streams, the river makes its way gently through the long valley of Rosedale which extends from the centre of the National Park to its southern perimeter. On reaching a gate, go diagonally across the field to a second gate. Follow the field edge, keeping the boundary on your immediate left, and make for a gate in the top corner. Continue ahead on a track and pass through two gates. Walk between farm outbuildings and return to the village of Appleton-le-Moors. Head up the main street towards the church, passing The Moors Inn on the left.

Cropton

Length of walk: 5¹/₂ miles
Start/finish: Cropton, north of the A170, between Pickering and Kirkbymoorside
Terrain: Muddy paths and tracks; several stretches of country road. Several short climbs

Glorious walk exploring the valley of the River Seven. Starting in the village of Cropton, the route crosses the wooded valley slopes to Lower Askew. Lying on the limestone upland east of Rosedale, the village of Cropton is famous for its pretty stone cottages and red pantiles. Many of these cottages date from the 18th and 19th centuries and some were rebuilt from earlier cruck houses and longhouses – two still have medieval crucks. The Victorian church of St Gregory is noted for its 12th century font and medieval window and part of an ancient cross stands in the churchyard. Behind the church lie the mound and ditch of a Norman castle.

From the unusually broad main street in Cropton, once used for grazing, make for the triangular green on the western side of the village. Turn left in the direction of Pickering and Wrelton and pass The New Inn. Swing right just beyond it, by the Cropton village sign, and follow a bridleway track known as Bull Ing Lane. Pass an isolated stone cottage and now the track dwindles to a grassy path.

Take the first of two gates side by side on the right and follow the path down between banks of undergrowth and trees. The path can be very wet and muddy throughout the year. Make for two gates and join a track running down to some double gates. On reaching a junction beyond them, swing left and follow the track to a footpath sign. Turn right for Appleton-le-Moors and follow the path down to the Seven riverbank. Cross the footbridge and turn left, skirting the field to a gate by the buildings of Appleton Mill Farm. Turn right and now there is a superb view. Keep to the muddy track as it hugs woodland on the left.

Eventually the path leaves the field edge and begins to ascend the valley slopes. Keep right at the fork and the River Seven can be seen down below through the trees. Take care as this stretch of the path is unfenced and there is a sharp drop on the right. Further on, the river can be seen sweeping away to the right. Continue on the path between the trees and gradually it begins to descend towards open farmland ahead. Go through the gate and follow the fence and hedge boundary, keeping it on the right. Make for the next boundary and stile and continue ahead to the road at Lower Askew.

Turn right and cross the road bridge, bearing right at the next junction for Rosedale and Pickering. Cross the River Seven at the next bridge, follow the road round the right-hand bend and press on through the countryside to Larchwood House and Beckhouse Farm. Turn right at the next junction and head towards Cropton, crossing the Cropton Beck. Follow the road up the hill until you see a track and a seat on the right. Take the track, muddy in places, and follow it to a turning on the right for Cropton Mill. Avoid the drive and continue ahead on Low Lane. Pass a path on the left and at the next junction of tracks, turn left and head up to Bull Ing Lane. Bear left on reaching it and retrace your steps to Cropton.

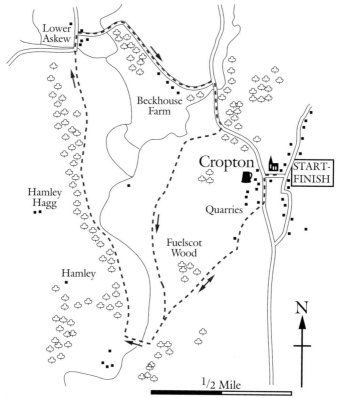

Marton and Normanby

> **Length of walk: 3 miles**
> **Start/finish: Marton village centre, south of the A170 between**
> **Pickering and Kirkbymoorside**
> **Terrain: Field paths and bridleways; brief stretches of country road.**
> **One gentle climb**

Pleasant lowland walk which heads south from the village of Marton to neighbouring Normanby before following a stretch of the meandering River Seven.

Marton, which was originally an agricultural settlement, lies within a wide loop of the River Seven and includes many houses built of Spaunton quarry limestone. That part of the village which is situated within the boundary of the river is a conservation area.

From the centre of the village, make for The Appletree Inn, cross the road by the sign and negotiate a stile between houses. Cross a paddock to a stile and make for a footbridge in the corner of the next paddock. Aim diagonally right in the next field; if it has recently been ploughed, then it is easier to follow the field boundary. Make for the far right corner where an obvious gap enables you to pass into the adjacent field.

Go straight ahead to a sign advising that all dogs must be kept on leads. Turn right and follow the track alongside a line of trees. Keep going until you see a bridleway track crossing your path immediately before a boundary hedge on the right. Bear left at this point and cut through the tongue of woodland to follow the left boundary of the field. Head up the slope to a gate in the top boundary and then continue straight ahead in the next field, keeping the hedge on the left. Go through the gate in the top corner of the field and then veer oblique right, with the buildings of Hill Top Farm clearly seen at this stage.

A good country walk usually springs one or two surprises and this circuit is

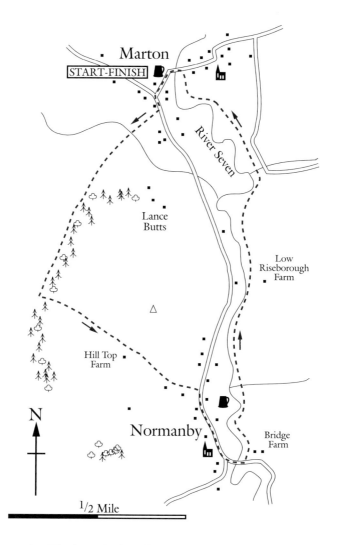

no exception. The dramatic view of the Vale of Pickering may well take your breath away as you suddenly find yourself looking out over a vast patchwork of distant trees, hedgerows and endless field patterns stretching as far as the eye can see. It is certainly a memorable and impressive scene.

Descend the slope, passing under power cables, and go through a wrought iron kissing gate to follow a path between fence and hedgerow. Drop down to a gate and note a property with some greenhouses on the right. Bear right and follow the road through the village of Normanby. Dating back to Norman times, Normanby was originally a resting place for travellers and their horses making the journey from Teesside to the Humber. At one time there were more than twelve hostelries in the village. The parish church of St Andrew is 12th century and, before mains water was brought to Normanby, the men of the village used to make their way through the churchyard and across the field to the river to fill their buckets with water which their wives then used on washdays.

Pass the church and the Sun Inn. On the right, just beyond the pub, is Normanby's old Wesleyan chapel, dated 1879. Follow the road over the bridge spanning the River Seven and veer round to the left. At the next right-hand bend turn left by Bridge House Farm and cross the grass to a gate and stile.

Join the grassy embankment and make for a stile and gate, keeping the Seven over to the left. Continue ahead in the next field, keeping to the embankment. Head for the next gate, avoiding a footbridge over to the left, and look for a stile up ahead at the next farm. Continue ahead, following the line of the embankment to the next stile. Beyond it, keep to the field edge and head for the road at a bend. Go straight ahead for about 30 yards, turning left at the stile and gate. Once in the field, veer right and go diagonally across the grass, aiming to the left of the distant silo.

Rejoin the embankment and make for a stile well to the left of farm outbuildings. Follow a grassy path running close to the riverbank, cross another stile and then turn right at a gate. Skirt the field to pass through two gates before reaching the road. Bear left and head back into the centre of Marton.

Wrelton and Beadale Valley

Length of walk: 2¹/₂ miles
Start/finish: Wrelton, located on the A170 between Pickering
and Kirkbymoorside
Terrain: Firm road surface and field path on the outward leg;
woodland paths, which can get muddy after rain and overgrown in
summer, on the return leg. Initial ascent out of the village

Short, easy walk which heads north out of Wrelton along a quiet country lane, returning to the start through the delightful tree-shaded Beadale Valley.

It may look like scores of other rural communities to the outsider but the village of Wrelton boasts a fascinating past. After the last Ice Age, when this entire area was submerged by floodwater, the village was a simple settlement clinging to the edge of the lake of Pickering. Much later, during the Roman Occupation, Wrelton occupied a key position on the route between Malton (Derventia) and Wade's Causeway on Stape Moor, and during the Georgian era, coaches would have stopped here on their way to Scarborough and Whitby.

From the centre of Wrelton go up Main Street towards Cropton and Hartoft. Pass rows of stone cottages and more modern houses before reaching the green on the right. Continue on up the hill towards the edge of the village, bending left further up. Turn immediately right after the bend and take the road for Cawthorne. Continue up the slope, passing some houses on the right. Once clear of Wrelton, follow the lane between hedgerows and banks. Glancing back at intervals reveals far-reaching views of the Vale of Pickering. From this impressive vantage point, a vast patchwork of fields, farms and hedgerows can be seen stretching away to the west.

When the road levels out, keep going between trees and hedgerows, fields and light woodland. Pass a turning for Crook Farm and Rocklands Nurseries on the left and continue along the lane between the remains of crumbling drystone walls. When you see a public bridleway sign on the right, leave the road and follow the vague path across the field, making for a distant curtain of woodland. Aim for a gate in the fence, directly in front of the trees, and follow the path, very slippery after rain, down through the undergrowth and vegetation of the Beadale Valley. After the vulnerability of the open ground, the soothing calm of the sheltered, dry valley is most welcome.

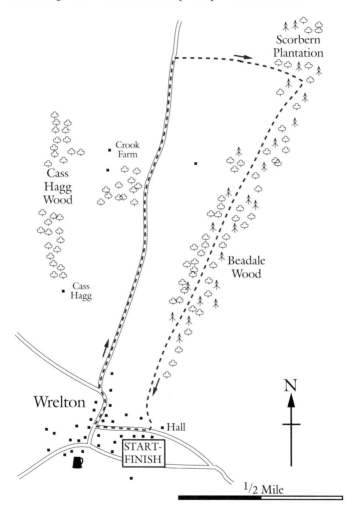

Turn right at the bottom of the bank, at the junction with the footpath and the bridleway, and follow the right of way along the valley floor. The path can get somewhat overgrown in places in high summer, though it is never impenetrable. Pick your way beneath the overhanging branches of trees and between margins of brambles and bracken. Your footsteps may even flush out the odd deer and, with a bit of luck, you might just catch sight of them moving swiftly between the trees.

The valley broadens out further on and the slopes can be seen studded with trees. When the path forks, avoid the upper trail running up out of the valley and keep to the lower route. Continue through the mixed woodland and between clumps of bracken, the path more easily defined along this stretch. At length, you can spot shafts of light through the trees ahead and soon you reach the edge of the woodland at the southern end of the valley.

Cross a stile and follow the grassy path ahead. Cross a second stile and skirt the field to its corner. The houses of Wrelton are visible now. Cross a third stile and go up the grassy path, keeping a wall on the right. Cross a fourth stile by a gate and join a track running to the road. Turn sharp right and walk back into Wrelton, passing the Methodist chapel and lines of picturesque, creeper-covered cottages as you go.

The first chapel to be built in Wrelton was the Wesleyan early in the 19th century. The Primitive Methodist followed in 1840. Both chapels were open every night of the week, playing a key role in the day-to-day life of the village. Social misfits and poverty-stricken members of the community were always given a warm welcome. Donations enabled food to be served, prepared and cooked in an old coal-fired copper, and the chapels even had their own small orchestras and choirs.

Publisher's Note
The information given in this book has been provided in good faith and is intended only as a general guide. Whilst all reasonable efforts have been made to ensure that details were correct at the time of publication, the author and Dalesman Publishing Company Ltd cannot accept any responsibility for inaccuracies. It is the responsibility of individuals undertaking outdoor activities to approach the activity with caution and, especially if inexperienced, to do so under appropriate supervision. They should also carry the appropriate equipment and maps, be properly clothed and have adequate footwear. The sport described in this book is strenuous and individuals should ensure that they are suitably fit before embarking upon it.